2017
Merry Christmas
Lauren
Lots of Love,
Ann & Tony

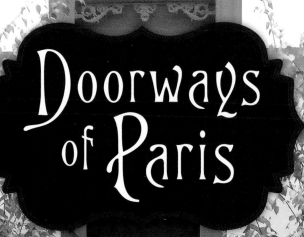

Doorways of Paris

PHOTOGRAPHS by RAQUEL PUIG

PROSPECT PARK BOOKS

Contents

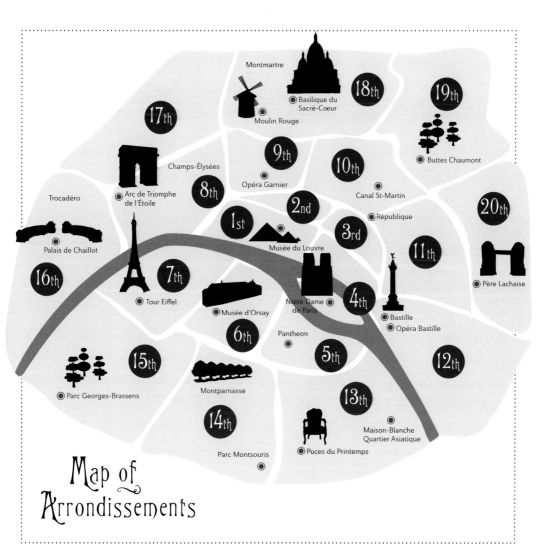

Map of Arrondissements

Montmartre

Basilique du Sacré-Cœur

Moulin Rouge

18th

19th

17th

Buttes Chaumont

9th

10th

Champs-Élysées

Opéra Garnier

Canal St-Martin

Trocadéro

Arc de Triomphe de l'Étoile

8th

2nd

20th

République

1st

3rd

Musée du Louvre

11th

Palais de Chaillot

16th

7th

Notre Dame de Paris

4th

Père Lachaise

Tour Eiffel

Musée d'Orsay

Bastille

Opéra Bastille

6th

Pantheon

5th

12th

Parc Georges-Brassens

15th

Montparnasse

13th

14th

Maison-Blanche
Quartier Asiatique

Parc Montsouris

Puces du Printemps

There are things known
and things unknown,
and in between are the doors.

—JIM MORRISON

In April of 2016, on an evening like so many others,
Vincent and I went for a stroll around our Paris
neighborhood, near Jardin de Luxembourg. Halfway
through, he stopped in front of a building and said,
"Look, such a gorgeous door." Indeed it was.

A few weeks later, it was me who was the one pointing
at a new door, telling him, "Look, this door looks like the
one you showed me." Something had clicked. I can't
really say why, but I started taking pictures of doors
here and there as a humble way to capture
the beauty of Paris.

Vincent suggested I open an Instagram account,
first of all so I wouldn't lose the photos (no matter how
far-sighted I am, he sees farther), but mostly because he
thought it would be a lovely way to share the timeless
gallery of doors that had begun to fascinate me.

Since that day, I've walked countless Parisian streets
in all twenty of the city's arrondissements, discovering
hidden gems and lovely landscapes that I never
imagined existed. The doors have become like my own
private city guides—guides who know everything, have
seen everything, and whisper of what is yet to come.
And along the way, I've encountered random wonderful
people who've told me stories about their neighborhoods, the history their doors have seen,
and the future they hope to see.

The door on the cover of this book might not be the
most magnificent one in Paris, or the most photo-
graphed one, but it is "our door." It's the one Vincent
showed me that spring day, the one that made me want
to explore each arrondissement in search of another
beautiful door, and the one that made me realize that
cities can be seen in endless fascinating ways. It's the
door that confirmed why I am more and more in love
with this man—and the city that watched him grow up.

I hope you enjoy strolling through these pages as
much as I enjoyed strolling the streets of Paris to
take the photographs.

For Vincent. From Paris. With love.

—RAQUEL PUIG

1st Arrondissement

The 1st arrondissement, in the heart of Paris, is one of the smallest and least populated areas of the city, home to such landmarks as the Louvre, the Tuileries, and the Palais-Royal, as well as offices and government buildings. So the doorways tend, of course, toward the old, ornate, and/or grand.

110 RUE DE RIVOLI · 5 RUE VILLÉDO
96 RUE SAINT-DENIS · 1 RUE THÉRÈSE

<<< 28 BIS RUE DE RICHELIEU

45 RUE SAINT-ROCH
3 & 5 PLACE ANDRÉ-MALRAUX

The fanciful combination of polished and painted metalwork and opulent floral-themed stonework at 16 rue du Louvre is an art nouveau treasure that was built in 1910–12 as part of the La Samaritaine complex. Make sure to take a look when visiting the nearby Louvre.

16 RUE DU LOUVRE

22 RUE DU COLONEL-DRIANT · 39 RUE DES PETITS-CHAMPS
296 RUE SAINT-HONORÉ (ÉGLISE SAINT-ROCH) · 92 RUE SAINT-DENIS (ÉGLISE SAINT-LEU)
2 PLACE DES PYRAMIDES (HÔTEL REGINA) · 5 AVENUE DE L'OPÉRA

Arches, arches everywhere, from the sacred to the commercial. Both churches are historic and deserve a visit; look for bullet holes dating to the French Revolution on the exterior of Saint-Roch (fun fact: the Marquis de Sade was married here in 1763), and for the crypt holding relics of Saint Helena, the empress responsible for spreading early Christianity, at the Gothic Saint-Leu.

20 QUAI DE LA MÉGISSERIE
10–12 QUAI DE LA MÉGISSERIE

2nd Arrondissement

The 2nd is home not only to the Opéra and the Bourse, but also to many of the city's remaining covered passageways, including Galerie Vivienne. Make sure to walk through the Galerie's iron doorway to experience the vaulted skylit ceilings and ornate tile floors, and by all means have a meal at Le Bougainville.

38 RUE TIQUETONNE

4 RUE DES PETITS-CHAMPS >>>

5 RUE D'ANTIN

32 AVENUE DE L'OPÉRA
20 RUE BACHAUMONT

Take a close look at 6 rue de Hanovre, an art nouveau beauty designed by
Bocage & Brilot. Not only is the doorway's metalwork extraordinary, but
the exterior tilework is stunning, and if you can get inside (it's an office
building) to see the lobby and stairway, you won't be sorry.

6 RUE DE HANOVRE

1 RUE LÉON-CLADEL · 61-63 RUE RÉAUMUR
1 BIS BOULEVARD DES ITALIENS · 60 RUE D'ARGOUT

Although the 2nd is best known for its grand, institutional buildings, it has its share of *charmant* apartment buildings as well. Each of these vibrant doorways leads to residences, typically above a restaurant or shop.

88 RUE MONTORGUEIL · 14 RUE CHABANAIS
17 RUE DU CROISSANT · 10 PLACE DES VICTOIRES

1 RUE CHERUBINI >>>

3rd Arrondissement

The rue de Turenne runs through the heart of the Marais, and a stroll along its length is an excellent way to get a feel for both the 3rd and 4th arrondissements. If you're lucky, a few doors like the one above will be open so you can peek into some ancient courtyards.

50 RUE DE TURENNE

<<< 254 RUE SAINT-MARTIN (ÉGLISE SAINT-NICOLAS-DES-CHAMPS)

The stately arched double doors at 110 rue Vieille-du-Temple lead
to the former Hôtel d'Hozier, a family palace begun in 1623 but not
completed for another century. The sculpture overhead is the
family crest of one of the early owners.

4 RUE RAMBUTEAU · 110 RUE VIEILLE-DU-TEMPLE
18 RUE COMMINES · 77 RUE DES GRAVILLIERS

Sometimes called the "upper Marais," the 3rd is rich in ancient streets, vibrant doorways, and museums crammed full of history, including the Carnavalet, the Arts et Métiers, the Archives, and our favorite, the Musée de la Chasse et de la Nature.

105-107 RUE VIEILLE-DU-TEMPLE · 106 RUE VIEILLE-DU-TEMPLE
225 RUE SAINT-MARTIN · 83 RUE DE TURENNE

A decade ago, Alain Maître Barbier Coiffeur was the last traditional barbershop left in Paris.
Now, however, barbershops are in vogue, with new ones all over town. But Alain's,
at 8 rue Saint-Claude in the heart of the Marais, is the only truly authentic one.

14 RUE SAINT-CLAUDE · 12 RUE SAINT-CLAUDE
103 BOULEVARD BEAUMARCHAIS · 8 RUE SAINT-CLAUDE

The diversity of the 3rd is evident in its doorways. The quarter blends 17th-century bourgeois residences with historically grand structures, like the Musée Carnavalet at 23 rue Sévigné—and plenty of the boldly artistic for character.

53 RUE DE MONTMORENCY · 57 BOULEVARD BEAUMARCHAIS
51 RUE MONTMORENCY · 23 RUE DE SÉVIGNÉ

4th Arrondissement

The 4th comprises three famous neighborhoods: the Île Saint-Louis, the eastern part of the Île de la Cité (including Notre Dame), and the Marais. The painted door on rue Pavée acknowledges the Marais's Jewish identity. Allow time on your 4th ramblings to visit Au Petit Versailles du Marais—the opera cakes, raspberry tarts, and croissants inside are every bit as lovely as the doorway's exterior promises.

RUE PAVÉE · 29 RUE DU ROI-DE-SICILE
6 RUE FERDINAND-DUVAL · 46 RUE DES ARCHIVES

1 RUE TIRON >>>

FRANÇAIS SOUVENEZ-VOUS
ICI
A ÉTÉ TUÉ Charles PEZIN
BRIGADIER
DES GARDIENS DE LA PAIX F.F.I.
LE 20 AOUT 1944

AU PETIT VERSAILLES DU MARAIS

Christian VABRET
Meilleur Ouvrier de France

5 RUE DES DEUX-PONTS

Red doors brighten gray winter days in the Marais. Across the street from 22 rue Beautreillis, at number 17, is the elegant apartment building in which Jim Morrison lived with his girlfriend Pamela Courson— and in which he died in 1971.

22 RUE BEAUTREILLIS · 17 RUE DU BOURG-TIBOURG
13 RUE CHARLES-V · 47 RUE VIEILLE-DU-TEMPLE

In the heart of the Marais sits the oldest planned square in Paris, the famed Place des Vosges, built by Henri IV in the early 1600s. Door lovers will want to take their time exploring the solid, simply elegant doorways framed by vaulted arcades.

18 PLACE DES VOSGES

In the 4th, old Paris survives on almost every block. This red-doored confection on the quai des Célestins near the Pont de Sully dates to the late 16th century. It was significantly renovated in the 17th century by famed architect Jules Hardouin-Mansart, and then again in 1857 by the Count of Lavelette and his architect, Jules Gros, who added some baroque Spanish-Italian flair. It's now a historic monument.

QUAI DES CÉLESTINS

Two green doors are found around
the corner from each other on the tiny,
quiet Île Saint-Louis. The island was
created in 1612 by connecting two
natural islets in the Seine, and in
the next few decades it was mapped
and developed as an elegant
neighborhood. It has remained just
that for 400 years.

27 RUE DES DEUX-PONTS · 39 RUE SAINT-LOUIS-EN-L'ÎLE

This ancient doorway is basically the service entrance to the building housing one of the city's oldest restaurants, Au Vieux Paris d'Arcole. This was the residence for priests from Notre Dame from 1512 until 1723, when it became a wine bar.

24 RUE CHANOINESSE

51 RUE SAINT-LOUIS-EN-L'ÎLE

30 RUE DE RIVOLI

5th Arrondissement

The 5th got its nickname, the Quartier Latin, because a few centuries back it was a university town where everyone spoke the universal language of academia, Latin. It varies from the ancient (the 5th was built as the Roman town Lutetia in the first century BC), to the sublime (the history, the doorways, the duck confit), to the touristy (the crowded area east of place Saint-Michel). To wallow in the history, visit Musée de Cluny, aka the National Museum of the Middle Ages.

6 PLACE PAUL-PAINLEVÉ (MUSÉE DE CLUNY)

<<< 107 RUE MONGE

The 5th is rich with ancient streets and gorgeous doors. Don't miss the one at 34 rue des Boulangers, which leads into a 17th-century townhouse where, so the story goes, the Marquise de Montespan, Louis XIV's most famous mistress, sent their many illegitimate children to be wet-nursed.

112-114 RUE MONGE · 82 RUE MONGE
62 RUE GAY-LUSSAC · 34 RUE DES BOULANGERS

It is not necessary to dine at Tour d'Argent (Silver Tower) at 15 quai de la Tournelle to appreciate its culinary and historic significance—a few minutes of admiring its doorway and marquise will do the trick. It's hard to believe now, but an 1860 guide to Paris called the restaurant "out of the way" and "cheap."

28 RUE SAINT-JACQUES · 15 QUAI DE LA TOURNELLE
3 RUE LE GOFF · 48 RUE MONGE

4 RUE D'ULM

One of the joys of the 5th is how you can go from the grand, bustling, and moneyed, as typified by the doorway at 21 boulevard Saint-Germain, to the quiet, hidden, and charming, like the red doorway on tiny rue Champollion.

41 RUE JUSSIEU · 26 RUE GAY-LUSSAC
21 BOULEVARD SAINT-GERMAIN · 12 RUE CHAMPOLLION

32-34 RUE GAY-LUSSAC · 27 RUE JUSSIEU
20 RUE CUVIER · 6 RUE DE POISSY
119 RUE MONGE · 38 BIS BOULEVARD SAINT-MARCEL

44 RUE GAY-LUSSAC

6ᵗʰ Arrondissement

Ah, the romance of the 6th! The Hemingways and Fitzgeralds lived and drank here, and Simone de Beauvoir and Jean-Paul Satre bonded here. To pay homage to the area's literary heritage, visit the glorious used bookshop at 62 rue de Vaugirard. The golden bulls' heads flanking the doorways are remnants of the building's previous incarnation as a Belle Epoque butcher shop. A few doors away, at number 58 (shown a few pages later), is the building that once housed the Fitzgeralds.

24 RUE DE SEINE · 62 RUE DE VAUGIRARD

7 RUE GUÉNÉGAUD >>>

36 RUE GUYNEMER

You'll find every kind of blue adorning the doorways of the 6th. Speaking of every kind of blue, jazz master Miles Davis loved Paris as much as Paris loved him. He often stayed in the 6th, at Hôtel La Louisiane on rue de Seine.

106 BIS RUE DE RENNES · 184 BOULEVARD SAINT-GERMAIN
45 RUE BONAPARTE · 72 BIS RUE BONAPARTE

Sometimes a remarkable doorway signifies a building of noteworthy design or history, as is the case with 98 rue du Cherche-Midi, where composer Maurice Jaubert once lived, and 9 rue Auguste-Comte, a lovely Moorish-inspired building that houses the École National d'Administration. And sometimes it has nothing whatsoever to do with its surrounding structure, as is the case with 27 rue Saint-Sulpice, whose doorway appears to be the sole survivor of an earlier building on this site.

27 RUE SAINT-SULPICE · 26 RUE GUYNEMER
82 RUE NOTRE-DAME-DES-CHAMPS · 9 RUE AUGUSTE-COMTE

98 RUE DU CHERCHE-MIDI

Rue Monsieur-le-Prince dates back to the early 1400s; the buildings with the addresses from 2 to 10 on one side of the street and 9 to 21 on the other were built in the late 1600s. Rue Le Verrier was named for the French astronomer Urbain Le Verrier, a regular at the nearby L'Observatoire de Paris in the 19th century.

65 RUE MONSIEUR-LE-PRINCE · 9-11 RUE MONSIEUR-LE-PRINCE
12 RUE LE VERRIER · 6 RUE LE VERRIER

Scott and Zelda Fitzgerald chose 58 rue de Vaugirard not because of its exceptional doorway, but because it's across the street from the Jardin du Luxembourg, where their daughter, Scottie, often played. Another doorway worthy of close examination is 18 rue du Cherche-Midi, part of a 1738 building designed by Claude Bonneau. Stand back to take in the majesty of the carved wood, then move in close to admire the iron knocker.

58 RUE DE VAUGIRARD · 7 RUE AUGUSTE-COMTE
18 RUE DU CHERCHE-MIDI · 10 RUE HONORÉ-CHEVALIER

7th Arrondissement

It doesn't get much more grandiosely French than in the 7th, where the Eiffel Tower, Invalides, Musée d'Orsay, and Musée Rodin (among others) compete for attention. (Sometimes, however, the doorways to the classically beautiful buildings in the 7th lead merely to chiropractors or dentists.) A bracing change of pace awaits pilgrims to the former home of beloved French singer Serge Gainsbourg at 5 rue de Verneuil, which has become a graffiti shrine.

14 AVENUE DE BRETEUIL · 2 RUE DE SOLFÉRINO
19 AVENUE DUQUESNE · 5 RUE DE VERNEUIL

<<< 25 QUAI ANATOLE FRANCE

Wedged between two typically imposing quai-front buildings overlooking the Seine is 13-15 quai Voltaire, supposedly the narrowest building in Paris. The towering blue doorway spans almost the entire width of the building.

13-15 QUAI VOLTAIRE

1 PLACE DU PRÉSIDENT-MITHOUARD · 24 AVENUE BOSQUET
18 AVENUE DE BRETEUIL · 11 RUE PERRONET

David Sedaris fans, note that inside 46 rue du Bac
is Deyrolle, the home décor and taxidermy shop that
he adores and Hugh loathes.

18 RUE DE BELLECHASSE
46 RUE DU BAC

Young Napoléon Bonaparte was a student at the École Militaire at 21 place Joffre, and it remains a military school today. It opens for public tours once a year in September, during European Heritage Days.

19 RUE DE VARENNE
21 PLACE JOFFRE

3 SQUARE RAPP · 151 RUE DE GRENELLE

Although today many consider it to have Paris's most stunning door, 29 avenue Rapp was quite the *scandale* when it was built in 1901. Architect Jules Lavirotte and ceramicist Alexandre Bigot used abundant sexual imagery, and the door is a phallic symbol, which few realize today. *Atlas Obscura* calls the building "a steam-punk aphrodisiac factory." The other two exuberant art nouveau fancies seen here are also their creations; one is just around the corner on square Rapp, and the other is a few blocks away on rue de Grenelle.

29 AVENUE RAPP

8th Arrondissement

The 8th is all about pomp and circumstance—it's home to the Arc de Triomphe, the Champs-Élysées, and the president's palace—and it's also a hub of commerce. Many of the jaw-dropping doors in the 8th, like the Second Empire carved beauty at 51 rue de Miromesnil, house offices; other addresses of note on that street are 66, where Jean-Luc Godard lived; 125, the former home of Napoleon Bonaparte's sister Elisa; 6, where Colette had a hair salon in the 1930s; and 77, where Nicolas Sarkozy keeps an office. You'll want to stroll along avenue Montaigne, where many doorways open into famed haute couture showrooms.

64 RUE DE MIROMESNIL · 63 RUE LA BOÉTIE · 7 AVENUE MONTAIGNE

51 RUE DE MIROMESNIL >>>

Paris's beauty has much to do with symmetry—the perfectly balanced twin doors, the flanking windows, the proportioned-just-so pair of light fixtures. But what makes the doorway at 9 avenue Montaigne one of the loveliest in all the city is the asymmetry of the petite door on the left. Who wouldn't want to use the servants' entrance at this *maison*?

7 RUE CLÉMENT-MAROT (HOTEL WEST-END)
9 AVENUE FRANKLIN D. ROOSEVELT · 5 AVENUE MONTAIGNE

9 AVENUE MONTAIGNE

6 RUE MARBEUF

From elite boutiques to international banks, the making of money reigns in the 8th, so it seems fitting to find so many gilt doorways. Sometimes the gold is minimalist, like at the Credit Industriel et Commercial building, and sometimes it goes for broke, like at 64 rue de Rome, currently home to the swank design firm Malherbe.

12 AVENUE MONTAIGNE · 64 RUE DE ROME
8 RUE DE TURIN · PLACE DE BEYROUTH

The purple doorway at 92 rue de Miromesnil brings Prince to mind.
And who doesn't want that?

92 RUE DE MIROMESNIL

5 RUE DE RIGNY
33 RUE LA BOÉTIE

9th Arrondissement

You could do far, far worse than to sit for a spell at one of the sidewalk cafés flanking the doorway to 4 place Gustave-Toudouze, looking onto a tree-shaded pedestrian street of tranquility and elegance. The building's architectural significance has earned it a spot on the city's list of historic monuments. Also a historic monument (the 9th is rich with them) is 22 rue de Douai, which was the home of Proust's friend Geneviève Halévy and her husband, composer Georges Bizet, in the 19th century.

4 PLACE GUSTAVE-TOUDOUZE

<<< 22 RUE DE DOUAI

Before you explore the rue des Martyrs and its surrounding streets, do yourself a favor and read Elaine Sciolino's book *The Only Street in Paris: Life on the Rue des Martyrs.* If you read it from a shady spot on place Saint-Georges, so much the better.

30 & 32 PLACE SAINT-GEORGES
51 RUE DES MARTYRS

Over the centuries, rue Henry-Monnier has housed painter
Jules Dupré, poet Louise Colet, composer Sebastián Iradier,
and filmmaker François Truffaut (actually, his grandparents,
with whom he lived for a while).

9 RUE HENRY-MONNIER
36 RUE PIERRE-FONTAINE (TIMHOTEL)

1 RUE CARDINAL-MERCIER · 17 RUE DE LA VICTOIRE
2 PLACE GUSTAVE-TOUDOUZE · 3 BIS RUE D'ATHÈNES

Rue Notre-Dame-de-Lorette begins at the early
19th-century church of the same name, where
Claude Monet was baptized.

14 RUE NOTRE-DAME-DE-LORETTE
38 RUE NOTRE-DAME-DE-LORETTE

Every Parisian doorway deserves a crown, none more so than 30 rue de Londres,
a glazed-tile beauty that was once the home of the Society of French Mineral Waters.
Look up to notice the cascading "water" tilework flanking the windows.

8 RUE DES MARTYRS · 30 RUE DE LONDRES
65 RUE CONDORCET · 43 RUE DU FAUBOURG MONTMARTE

Plan to stand back and study the stunner that is 18 rue de Londres, a mansion built in 1883 by architect Jacques Drevet for the world-famous actress Anna Judic. Note the spectacular stained glass on the second floor. Alas, a mere decade later she was forced to sell the house after her career nosedived.

12 RUE CARDINAL-MERCIER · 34 RUE DE CLICHY
18 RUE DE LONDRES · 12 RUE DE CLICHY

10ᵗʰ Arrondissement

It's hip and happening in the 10th, home to much of the Canal Saint-Martin, two train stations, Gare du Nord and Gare de l'Est, and a vibrant café culture. After the devastation of the 2015 terrorist attacks, the residents and businesses rebuilt, mourned, and got back to daily life in one of the city's most diverse, engaging, and "everyday" arrondissements.

5 RUE DES PETITS-HÔTELS · 9 RUE DE VALENCIENNES
57 RUE DE L'AQUEDUC · 29 RUE LUCIEN-SAMPAIX

171 RUE LA FAYETTE >>>

16 PLACE DE LA RÉPUBLIQUE

47 RUE D'ALSACE

17 PLACE DE LA RÉPUBLIQUE · 15 PLACE DE LA RÉPUBLIQUE

Nothing represents the Parisian architectural aesthetic more than these matched sets of doors. Please ignore the McDonald's, Quick, and Hippopotamus fast-food joints that adjoin some of these beauties, and instead imagine the serenity of the apartment you might call home, just through those doors and two or three floors above the fray.

36 RUE DES PETITS-HÔTELS · 29 RUE BEAUREPAIRE
9 BOULEVARD DE DENAIN · 148 RUE LA FAYETTE

11th Arrondissement

The 11th is having its moment—it's where Parisian millennials seek apartments and where in-the-know shoppers and café crawlers go to explore. This working-class area has just enough shabby to be chic, and just enough secret spots to give it an air of mystery. Perhaps the most magical secret spot is passage Lhomme, a leafy cobblestone lane hidden off busy rue de Charonne. It's lined with such ateliers as Hollard, a furniture restorer.

124 BOULEVARD VOLTAIRE · 44 RUE FAIDHERBE
5 RUE DE L'ASILE-POPINCOURT · 185 BOULEVARD VOLTAIRE

<<< PASSAGE LHOMME (OFF 26 RUE DE CHARONNE)

Even some of the less charming passages in the 11th hold surprises, like this stained-glass beauty on the narrow, ancient passage Lisa. Behind the blue door is the studio of the painter Philippe Massis.

8 BIS PASSAGE LISA

8 PASSAGE LHOMME

102 BOULEVARD BEAUMARCHAIS

Green and red, ornate and plain, stately and humble—
the doorways of the 11th represent the diversity
of the arrondissement.

64 BOULEVARD VOLTAIRE · 4 PASSAGE BASFROI
67 RUE DE CHARONNE · 46 BOULEVARD VOLTAIRE

166 BOULEVARD VOLTAIRE
31-33 RUE FAIDHERBE

Sometimes a Parisian doorway promises things that are no longer there, like the electrical supplies at 166 boulevard Voltaire. But sometimes you get exactly what you see, as with the pharmacy behind the medical-cross door on rue de la Roquette. This kind of novelty architecture is common in places like Los Angeles but is a rare treat in Paris.

166 RUE DE LA ROQUETTE

Less famous than the neighboring Marais, and less *au courant* than its other neighbor, the 11th, the 12th arrondissement is blessed with both wide-open beauty (the Bois de Vincennes) and cozy, everyday urbanity, like the twice-weekly market that crowds into place Lachambeaudie.

10 PLACE D'ALIGRE · 19 RUE D'ALIGRE
8 PLACE D'ALIGRE · 1 PLACE LACHAMBEAUDIE

4 RUE ERARD >>>

21 RUE CRÉMIEUX · 30 RUE CRÉMIEUX
8 RUE CRÉMIEUX · 7 RUE CRÉMIEUX
19 RUE CRÉMIEUX · 15 RUE CRÉMIEUX

Cobblestoned and car-free, short rue Crémieux is found between rue de Lyon and rue de Bercy. It represents the homey side of Paris that not everyone realizes exists. The paint jobs prove how proud the residents are of their little corner of Parisian paradise, but they deserve their privacy, so explorers, please be mindful.

23 RUE CRÉMIEUX

12 RUE THÉOPHILE-ROUSSEL

Each of these double doors is a work of art, but when you add their
carved stonework "frames," they become masterpieces.

41 AVENUE DE SAINT-MANDRÉ · 4 PLACE DU COLONEL-BOURGOIN
30 AVENUE DAUMESNIL · 14 AVENUE LEDRU-ROLLIN

5 PLACE LACHAMBEAUDIE

Behind the red doors stands at the ready the first company of the second brigade
of Paris's famed *sapeurs pompiers* (firefighters).

13th Arrondissement

Not for much longer will the 13th be under the radar. It's the home of a major new tech incubator, vibrant Asian communities, a superb collection of street art, and fetching residential enclaves in the Maison-Blanche and Butte-aux-Cailles quarters, where most of these doorways are found.

55 BOULEVARD ARAGO · 127 RUE DE LA GLACIÈRE
14 RUE ERNEST ET HENRI ROUSSELLE · PASSAGE SIGAUD

<<< 7 RUE DE L'INTERNE-LOEB

The narrow doorways on the even-numbered side of rue Henri-Pape
look the same for a reason—these homes were built identically for a
cooperative society called La Petite Chaumière in the early 20th century.

8 RUE HENRI-PAPE · 4 RUE HENRI-PAPE
14 RUE HENRI-PAPE · 12 RUE HENRI-PAPE

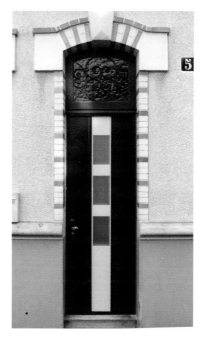

The history, the hominess, the diversity, the art of the 13th...
all are abundantly evident in its doorways.

10 BOULEVARD ARAGO · 30 RUE DE LA BUTTE-AUX-CAILLES
12 BOULEVARD ARAGO · 5 RUE ERNEST ET HENRI ROUSSELLE

If you can stroll the streets of La Cité Florale on the edge of the quartier Maison-Blanche in the late spring or summer, you'll get to revel in the lilacs, wisteria, roses, and irises that the streets are named after. This luscious residential enclave was built in the 1920s on the site of a large meadow whose underlying ground wasn't stable enough for building high-rises. Thank goodness.

6 RUE DES IRIS · 5 RUE DES ORCHIDÉES
15 RUE DES ORCHIDÉES · 7 RUE DES IRIS

8 RUE DES GLYCINES

14th Arrondissement

The 14th may be best known for Tour Montparnasse, the Catacombs, and Cimetière du Montparnasse, but for those of us who love it, it's all about the hidden residential enclaves. None exemplify this more than rue des Thermophyles and impasse du Moulin-Vert, where the cobblestones are substantial and the wisteria are plentiful.

RUE DES THERMOPHYLES
27 IMPASSE DU MOULIN-VERT

33 RUE DES THERMOPHYLES >>>

27 RUE JEAN-DOLENT

So many doorways to explore in the 14th! Do not miss square de
Montsouris, a stunning street of vine-clad art nouveau and art
deco houses. After some doorway exploring, a picnic in
the neighboring Parc Montsouris is just the thing.

SQUARE DE MONTSOURIS · SQUARE DE MONTSOURIS
4 RUE ASSELINE · RUE DES THERMOPHYLES

Man Ray had his studio in the spectacular tile-clad building at 31 rue Campagne-Première. Other former residents of this neighborhood around Cimetière du Montparnasse were Simone de Beauvoir (on rue Victor Schoelcher) and Jean-Paul Sartre (in the Hôtel Mistral on rue Cels); they are buried side by side in the cemetery.

31 RUE CAMPAGNE-PREMIÈRE · 12 SQUARE DELAMBRE
1 RUE BOULARD · 177 RUE D'ALÉSIA

Every proper community needs an intellectual hub, and the
14th is blessed with the Cité Internationale Universitaire de Paris,
a foundation that houses students and academics from all over
the world. These are but two of its many worthy doorways that
lead to international cooperation and learning.

17 BOULEVARD JOURDAN (PAVILLON PASTEUR)
17 BOULEVARD JOURDAN (FONDATION BIERMANS)

15th Arrondissement

Although the 15th has its share of unfortunate modern towers, it also has some art nouveau stunners, none more exceptional than Alfred Wagon's 1904 creation on place Étienne-Pernet. Make sure to stand back from across the street to take in the fabulously fanciful balconies, windows, and ornaments above the rare asymmetrical doorway. The other two doorways shown here are also art nouveau beauties; get up close to rue de la Convention so you can see the big jungle cat above the address.

18 RUE DU GÉNÉRAL-BEURET

170 RUE DE LA CONVENTION

<<< 24 PLACE ÉTIENNE-PERNET

Studies in brown, with a whimsical *chapeau,*
elegant lines, and ornate tilework.

16 RUE LÉON-DELHOMME · 176 RUE DE LA CONVENTION
4 RUE D'ARSONVAL · 7 RUE PÉTEL

Studies in blue, with meticulous ironwork, timeless symmetry,
and regularly refreshed paint.

20 RUE SAINTE-FÉLICITÉ · 11 RUE CHASSELOUP-LAUBAT
15 RUE GERBERT · 12 RUE CHASSELOUP-LAUBAT

Many of the doorways in the 15th evoke a comforting, old-fashioned hominess.
A favorite is the old house on rue Léon-Delhomme, which still has its old barn
attached—a rare sight indeed in this now-fully-urban environment.

10 RUE PÉTEL · 5 PASSAGE OLIVIER-DE-SERRES
17 RUE LÉON-DELHOMME · 109 RUE CAMBRONNE

50 AVENUE DE SÉGUR

Ah, the refinement, the elegance, the (let's just say it) wealth of the 16th...
all are evident in these superb ironwork doors, which typify the 19th-century
style of the district. There are so many reasons to visit the 16th, from the Musée
Marmottan and Stade Roland Garros to Fondation Le Corbusier and the Pont
de Bir-Hakeim. Just make sure to allow enough time to discover its doorways.

104 AVENUE RAYMOND-POINCARE
15 AVENUE PERRICHONT

90 AVENUE RAYMOND-POINCARE >>>

38 RUE NICOLO · 6 RUE COPERNIC
9 RUE DU PÈRE-BROTTIER · 50 AVENUE DU PRÉSIDENT-WILSON

From an elegant high school, to posh lawyers' offices, to
stately homes, the doorways of the 16th practically reek
of old money. Right across the street from 50 avenue du
Président-Wilson are the Jardins du Trocadéro, including
the Musée de l'Homme and the Paris Aquarium.

66 AVENUE KLÉBER
8 RUE CHARDON-LAGACHE

14 RUE JEAN DE LA FONTAINE (CASTEL BÉRANGER)

You simply cannot call yourself a Paris doorway aficionado until you have visited Castel Béranger, the first art nouveau residence in Paris. It was designed with exuberant whimsy by 27-year-old Hector Guimard, who went on to create many iconic Métro entrances (some of which were torn down when art nouveau fell out of fashion). The houses on rue Chardon-Lagache and rue Boileau are two more Guimard masterpieces, and they make apparent his influence on the American Arts & Crafts movement.

41 RUE CHARDON-LAGACHE · 2 RUE EUGÈNE-MANUEL
34 RUE BOILEAU · 14 RUE POUSSIN

It's typical to see a few art nouveau devotees standing raptly before the Hôtel Mezzara, built in 1910 by Hector Guimard, whose famed Castel Béranger is on the same street.

60 RUE JEAN DE LA FONTAINE (HÔTEL MEZZARA)
42 RUE DE L'YVETTE

After his riotous successes, art nouveau pioneer Guimard designed
every inch of the house at 122 avenue Mozart—down to the radiators
and doorknobs—for himself and his wife, American painter Adeline
Oppenheim. The two moved to New York in the late 1930s during the
rise of anti-Semitism in Paris, and Guimard died a forgotten genius.

3 RUE RENÉ-BAZIN
122 AVENUE MOZART

17th Arrondissement

Just three of the many graceful doorways along avenue de
Villiers in the 17th, a large, heavily residential arrondissement.
Number 89 was the home of Princess Marie Cantacuzène of
Romania, who, after two brief, unhappy marriages, was the
lifelong muse and mistress of artist Pierre Puvis de
Chavannes. He called on her every evening
at this house after a hard day's painting
in his Pigalle atelier.

83 AVENUE DE VILLIERS · 63 AVENUE DE VILLIERS

<<< 89 AVENUE DE VILLIERS

43 RUE DES DAMES

Is any city in the world blessed with more, and more beautiful, keystone art than Paris?
Here are but five examples of the thousands of gods, goddesses, creatures,
and artworks that reign over the doorways of Paris.

2 AVENUE DE VILLIERS · 90 AVENUE NIEL
18 AVENUE MAC-MAHON · 98 AVENUE NIEL

18th

Arrondissement

Dense and hilly and diverse, the 18th is known for its two main sections, Montmartre (the steeply pitched home of Sacre-Coeur) and Goutte d'Or, a diverse African and Afro-French community. Its doorways lead to both places of touristy legend (Au Lapin Agile) and hidden rusticity.

31 RUE LEPIC · 22 RUE DES SAULES (AU LAPIN AGILE)
27 RUE GABRIELLE · 11 RUE THOLOZÉ

25 RUE GABRIELLE >>>

24 RUE DES SAULES

Some of the greatest artists of the 19th and 20th centuries—Picasso, Van Gogh, Toulouse-Lautrec—frequented this old stone street, and some, like Paul Cézanne, painted it (*Rue des Saules, Montmartre,* 1867). So if you have an artistic bone in your body, you must experience this street. The charm of its doorways is a bonus.

26 RUE DES SAULES

While exploring rue de l'Abreuvoir, note the pink house at number 2, painted by many artists; the sundial at number 4; and the house at 15-16, which was the site of Montmartre's water trough for much of its history.

4 RUE DE L'ABREUVOIR
8 RUE DE L'ABREUVOIR

A stroll down Villa Léandre is like going to the country for the
weekend. Built on the site of a former mill, it was developed
in the 1920s as an homage to English architecture; note the
"Downing Street" sign at number 10.

6 VILLA LÉANDRE
10 VILLA LÉANDRE

Not only is the doorway to 20 rue Durantin a work of art, but it was also a portal that the painters Henry-Eugène Delacroix and Georges Delaw, who once had studios here, passed through daily. 13 place Émile-Goudeau, sharing a wall with number 11 bis, is the famed Bateau-Lavoir, a former residence and hangout for many of the leaders in art, literature, and theater in the early 20th century. While living here, Picasso painted *Les Demoiselles d'Avignon*. Can't top that.

43 RUE DURANTIN · 7 RUE FAUVET
27 RUE LEPIC · 11 BIS ÉMILE-GOUDEAU

20 RUE DURANTIN

19th Arrondissement

The 19th has never been the most glamorous part of Paris—in the 12th century it was home to a leper colony—but much has changed. It's hard to believe that the lovely Parc de la Villette was the site of the city's massive slaughterhouse as recently as 1974. The 19th also boasts many quiet, greenery-lined residential streets; make sure to explore the pedestrian-only "Villa" streets just east of the huge Parc des Buttes-Chaumont.

16 RUE DE MOUZAÏA · 7 VILLA DE LA RENAISSANCE
10 RUE DES MIGNOTTES · 44 RUE DE LA VILLETTE

<<< 10 VILLA EUGÈNE-LEBLANC

You'll find some doorways with a bit of grandeur
in the 19th, but most captivating are the friendly
ones leading into the old stone houses on the
little streets east of Buttes-Chaumont.

2 PLACE ARMAND-CARREL · 118 BIS RUE COMPANS
40 RUE DU GÉNÉRAL-BRUNET · 13 RUE MIGUEL-HIDALGO

14 RUE DE MOUZAÏA
17 RUE DE LA VILLETTE

The living and the dead share Paris's "last" arrondissement, known as the site of Père Lachaise cemetery, the resting place of so many luminaries, from Piaf to Pissarro, Molière to Morrison, Wright to Wilde. On the living side of town you'll find an appealingly everyday Paris, with almost no tourists and lots of families, including immigrants from West and North Africa, and two great markets: the Montreuil Flea Market and the North African Marché de Belleville.

FAMILLE MARLOT CRYPT, CIMETIÈRE DU PÈRE LACHAISE

6 CITÉ DES ÉCOLES >>>

"The passage from the big to the little is what makes Paris beautiful, and you have to be prepared to be small—to live, to trudge, to have your head down in melancholy and then lift it up, sideways—to get it."
—ADAM GOPNIK, *PARIS TO THE MOON*

"Blessed are they who see beautiful things in humble places where other people see nothing."
—CAMILLE PISSARRO

42 BIS RUE DES CASCADES · 70 RUE DES CASCADES
80 RUE DES CASCADES · 131 RUE DES PYRÉNÉES

"A walk about in Paris will provide lessons in history, beauty, and in the point of life."
—THOMAS JEFFERSON

"Paris is always a good idea."
—AUDREY HEPBURN IN *SABRINA*

75 RUE DE LA MARE · 8 CITÉ DES ÉCOLES
44 RUE DE LA BIDASSOA · 2 BIS RUE DES CASCADES

THIS IS THE END—THE DOORWAY INTO THE CATACOMBS,
14TH ARRONDISSSEMENT.

...

Photographs © 2017 by Raquel Puig

All rights reserved. No part of this book may be reproduced or transmitted in any form or by any
means, electronic or mechanical, including photocopying, recording, or by any information storage
and retrieval system, without permission in writing from the publisher.

Published by Prospect Park Books
2359 Lincoln Avenue
Altadena, California 91001
www.prospectparkbooks.com

Distributed by Consortium Books Sales & Distribution
www.cbsd.com

Library of Congress Cataloging in Publication Data is on file
with the Library of Congress. The following is for reference only:
Names: Puig, Raquel, photographer
Titles: Doorways of Paris (2017)
Identifiers: ISBN: 978-1-945551-06-2 (hardback)
Subjects: Paris (France)—Travel | Paris (France)—Photographs. | BISAC: TRAVEL / Europe / France

Text by Colleen Dunn Bates
Designed by Kathy Kikkert
First edition, first printing
Printed in China by Imago on sustainably produced,
FSC-certified paper